For more information:
info@ilemonbk.com
P.O. Box 50328
Brooklyn, NY 11205

FIRST EDITION

ISBN: 978-1-7366168-1-9

www.ilemonbk.com

MULANI MONEYBAGS
LEMONADE STAND JOURNAL

DATE	PRODUCT NAME (EXPENSE -)	COST	PRODUCT NAME (SALE +)	COST	PROFIT/ LOSS

MULANI MONEYBAGS
LEMONADE STAND JOURNAL

DATE	PRODUCT NAME (EXPENSE -)	COST	PRODUCT NAME (SALE +)	COST	PROFIT/ LOSS

MULANI MONEYBAGS
LEMONADE STAND JOURNAL

DATE	PRODUCT NAME (EXPENSE -)	COST	PRODUCT NAME (SALE +)	COST	PROFIT/ LOSS

MULANI MONEYBAGS
LEMONADE STAND JOURNAL

DATE	PRODUCT NAME (EXPENSE -)	COST	PRODUCT NAME (SALE +)	COST	PROFIT/ LOSS

MULANI MONEYBAGS
LEMONADE STAND JOURNAL

DATE	PRODUCT NAME (EXPENSE -)	COST	PRODUCT NAME (SALE +)	COST	PROFIT/ LOSS

MULANI MONEYBAGS
LEMONADE STAND JOURNAL

DATE	PRODUCT NAME (EXPENSE -)	COST	PRODUCT NAME (SALE +)	COST	PROFIT/ LOSS

MULANI MONEYBAGS
LEMONADE STAND JOURNAL

DATE	PRODUCT NAME (EXPENSE -)	COST	PRODUCT NAME (SALE +)	COST	PROFIT/ LOSS

MULANI MONEYBAGS
LEMONADE STAND JOURNAL

DATE	PRODUCT NAME (EXPENSE -)	COST	PRODUCT NAME (SALE +)	COST	PROFIT/ LOSS

MULANI MONEYBAGS
LEMONADE STAND JOURNAL

DATE	PRODUCT NAME (EXPENSE -)	COST	PRODUCT NAME (SALE +)	COST	PROFIT/ LOSS

MULANI MONEYBAGS
LEMONADE STAND JOURNAL

DATE	PRODUCT NAME (EXPENSE -)	COST	PRODUCT NAME (SALE +)	COST	PROFIT/ LOSS

MULANI MONEYBAGS
LEMONADE STAND JOURNAL

DATE	PRODUCT NAME (EXPENSE -)	COST	PRODUCT NAME (SALE +)	COST	PROFIT/ LOSS

MULANI MONEYBAGS
LEMONADE STAND JOURNAL

DATE	PRODUCT NAME (EXPENSE -)	COST	PRODUCT NAME (SALE +)	COST	PROFIT/ LOSS

MULANI MONEYBAGS
LEMONADE STAND JOURNAL

DATE	PRODUCT NAME (EXPENSE -)	COST	PRODUCT NAME (SALE +)	COST	PROFIT/ LOSS

MULANI MONEYBAGS
LEMONADE STAND JOURNAL

DATE	PRODUCT NAME (EXPENSE -)	COST	PRODUCT NAME (SALE +)	COST	PROFIT/ LOSS

MULANI MONEYBAGS
LEMONADE STAND JOURNAL

DATE	PRODUCT NAME (EXPENSE -)	COST	PRODUCT NAME (SALE +)	COST	PROFIT/ LOSS

MULANI MONEYBAGS
LEMONADE STAND JOURNAL

DATE	PRODUCT NAME (EXPENSE -)	COST	PRODUCT NAME (SALE +)	COST	PROFIT/ LOSS

MULANI MONEYBAGS
LEMONADE STAND JOURNAL

DATE	PRODUCT NAME (EXPENSE -)	COST	PRODUCT NAME (SALE +)	COST	PROFIT/ LOSS

MULANI MONEYBAGS
LEMONADE STAND JOURNAL

DATE	PRODUCT NAME (EXPENSE -)	COST	PRODUCT NAME (SALE +)	COST	PROFIT/ LOSS

MULANI MONEYBAGS
LEMONADE STAND JOURNAL

DATE	PRODUCT NAME (EXPENSE -)	COST	PRODUCT NAME (SALE +)	COST	PROFIT/ LOSS

MULANI MONEYBAGS
LEMONADE STAND JOURNAL

DATE	PRODUCT NAME (EXPENSE -)	COST	PRODUCT NAME (SALE +)	COST	PROFIT/ LOSS

MULANI MONEYBAGS
LEMONADE STAND JOURNAL

DATE	PRODUCT NAME (EXPENSE -)	COST	PRODUCT NAME (SALE +)	COST	PROFIT/ LOSS

MULANI MONEYBAGS
LEMONADE STAND JOURNAL

DATE	PRODUCT NAME (EXPENSE -)	COST	PRODUCT NAME (SALE +)	COST	PROFIT/ LOSS

MULANI MONEYBAGS
LEMONADE STAND JOURNAL

DATE	PRODUCT NAME (EXPENSE -)	COST	PRODUCT NAME (SALE +)	COST	PROFIT/ LOSS

MULANI MONEYBAGS
LEMONADE STAND JOURNAL

DATE	PRODUCT NAME (EXPENSE -)	COST	PRODUCT NAME (SALE +)	COST	PROFIT/ LOSS

MULANI MONEYBAGS
LEMONADE STAND JOURNAL

DATE	PRODUCT NAME (EXPENSE -)	COST	PRODUCT NAME (SALE +)	COST	PROFIT/ LOSS

MULANI MONEYBAGS
LEMONADE STAND JOURNAL

DATE	PRODUCT NAME (EXPENSE -)	COST	PRODUCT NAME (SALE +)	COST	PROFIT/ LOSS

MULANI MONEYBAGS
LEMONADE STAND JOURNAL

DATE	PRODUCT NAME (EXPENSE -)	COST	PRODUCT NAME (SALE +)	COST	PROFIT/ LOSS

MULANI MONEYBAGS
LEMONADE STAND JOURNAL

DATE	PRODUCT NAME (EXPENSE -)	COST	PRODUCT NAME (SALE +)	COST	PROFIT/ LOSS

MULANI MONEYBAGS
LEMONADE STAND JOURNAL

DATE	PRODUCT NAME (EXPENSE -)	COST	PRODUCT NAME (SALE +)	COST	PROFIT/ LOSS

MULANI MONEYBAGS
LEMONADE STAND JOURNAL

DATE	PRODUCT NAME (EXPENSE -)	COST	PRODUCT NAME (SALE +)	COST	PROFIT/ LOSS

MULANI MONEYBAGS
LEMONADE STAND JOURNAL

DATE	PRODUCT NAME (EXPENSE -)	COST	PRODUCT NAME (SALE +)	COST	PROFIT/ LOSS

MULANI MONEYBAGS
LEMONADE STAND JOURNAL

DATE	PRODUCT NAME (EXPENSE -)	COST	PRODUCT NAME (SALE +)	COST	PROFIT/ LOSS

MULANI MONEYBAGS
LEMONADE STAND JOURNAL

DATE	PRODUCT NAME (EXPENSE -)	COST	PRODUCT NAME (SALE +)	COST	PROFIT/ LOSS

MULANI MONEYBAGS
LEMONADE STAND JOURNAL

DATE	PRODUCT NAME (EXPENSE -)	COST	PRODUCT NAME (SALE +)	COST	PROFIT/ LOSS

MULANI MONEYBAGS
LEMONADE STAND JOURNAL

DATE	PRODUCT NAME (EXPENSE -)	COST	PRODUCT NAME (SALE +)	COST	PROFIT/ LOSS

MULANI MONEYBAGS
LEMONADE STAND JOURNAL

DATE	PRODUCT NAME (EXPENSE -)	COST	PRODUCT NAME (SALE +)	COST	PROFIT/ LOSS

MULANI MONEYBAGS
LEMONADE STAND JOURNAL

DATE	PRODUCT NAME (EXPENSE -)	COST	PRODUCT NAME (SALE +)	COST	PROFIT/ LOSS

MULANI MONEYBAGS
LEMONADE STAND JOURNAL

DATE	PRODUCT NAME (EXPENSE -)	COST	PRODUCT NAME (SALE +)	COST	PROFIT/ LOSS

MULANI MONEYBAGS
LEMONADE STAND JOURNAL

DATE	PRODUCT NAME (EXPENSE -)	COST	PRODUCT NAME (SALE +)	COST	PROFIT/ LOSS

MULANI MONEYBAGS
LEMONADE STAND JOURNAL

DATE	PRODUCT NAME (EXPENSE -)	COST	PRODUCT NAME (SALE +)	COST	PROFIT/ LOSS

MULANI MONEYBAGS
LEMONADE STAND JOURNAL

DATE	PRODUCT NAME (EXPENSE -)	COST	PRODUCT NAME (SALE +)	COST	PROFIT/ LOSS

MULANI MONEYBAGS
LEMONADE STAND JOURNAL

DATE	PRODUCT NAME (EXPENSE -)	COST	PRODUCT NAME (SALE +)	COST	PROFIT/ LOSS

MULANI MONEYBAGS
LEMONADE STAND JOURNAL

DATE	PRODUCT NAME (EXPENSE -)	COST	PRODUCT NAME (SALE +)	COST	PROFIT/ LOSS

MULANI MONEYBAGS
LEMONADE STAND JOURNAL

DATE	PRODUCT NAME (EXPENSE -)	COST	PRODUCT NAME (SALE +)	COST	PROFIT/ LOSS

MULANI MONEYBAGS
LEMONADE STAND JOURNAL

DATE	PRODUCT NAME (EXPENSE -)	COST	PRODUCT NAME (SALE +)	COST	PROFIT/ LOSS

MULANI MONEYBAGS
LEMONADE STAND JOURNAL

DATE	PRODUCT NAME (EXPENSE -)	COST	PRODUCT NAME (SALE +)	COST	PROFIT/ LOSS

MULANI MONEYBAGS
LEMONADE STAND JOURNAL

DATE	PRODUCT NAME (EXPENSE -)	COST	PRODUCT NAME (SALE +)	COST	PROFIT/ LOSS

MULANI MONEYBAGS
LEMONADE STAND JOURNAL

DATE	PRODUCT NAME (EXPENSE -)	COST	PRODUCT NAME (SALE +)	COST	PROFIT/ LOSS

MULANI MONEYBAGS
LEMONADE STAND JOURNAL

DATE	PRODUCT NAME (EXPENSE -)	COST	PRODUCT NAME (SALE +)	COST	PROFIT/ LOSS

MULANI MONEYBAGS
LEMONADE STAND JOURNAL

DATE	PRODUCT NAME (EXPENSE -)	COST	PRODUCT NAME (SALE +)	COST	PROFIT/ LOSS

Made in the USA
Monee, IL
04 November 2026

67379690R00030